Making the Modern World
Europe

Hitler

L. E. Snellgrove

Longman

Death in the Wolf's Lair

The Wolf's Lair after the explosion

It is a very hot day in July 1944. Twenty-four German officers are sitting at a table in a wooden hut. With them is Adolf Hitler. This room is part of his headquarters near Berlin—his Wolf's Lair, as he calls it. Around him are generals and other experts helping to plan the war against Russia, Britain and the United States.

One officer, Colonel Stauffenberg, is quite near Hitler. After a time he gets up and says to Colonel Brandt beside him, 'I must go and telephone. Keep an eye on my brief case. It has secret papers in it.' The case is on the floor, resting against a chair leg. It is only six feet from Hitler. Stauffenberg walks out. Brandt leans forward to look at a map on the table. His foot knocks against the case. He picks it up and puts it on the other side of a wooden post. This post is now between Hitler and the case. By moving it nearer to himself, Brandt has made certain that he will die because inside the case is a two-pound bomb, fused and ready to go off. The minutes tick away. A general is reading a report aloud. Inside the case, acid is eating through the thin wire of the fuse.

Ten minutes pass. One or two of the generals begin to wonder why Stauffenberg is so long at the phone. Suddenly there is a terrific explosion. Flashes of yellow flame and thick black smoke fill the room. The ceiling falls in; the table is smashed to bits; all the windows and part of one wall collapse. People are picked up and thrown about like dolls. Standing outside, Stauffenberg sees some bodies fly out of the window. When the smoke clears the room is a muddle of smashed wood. Bloodstained men with torn clothes stagger to their feet. One or two lie still on the floor.

Staffenberg is sure he has killed Hitler; no one, he thinks, could live after such an explosion. He leaves at once for Berlin to tell his friends that all is well. With Hitler dead, they can change the German government and make peace with Britain and the United States.

He has made a dreadful mistake. Only four of those in the room are dead or dying. Hitler himself has been saved by the thick post. The bomb blast threw him against the wall. It set fire to his hair as well as hurting his ear drums. His legs and back are bruised and burned. Afterwards he says he has 'a backside like a baboon'. But he is alive and furious that anyone should try to kill him.

Before evening of that day, Stauffenberg is captured and shot. He is lucky. Many of the men in the plot die a horrible death. Hitler has them hanged by piano wire from meat hooks. They strangle slowly. A film is made of the scene so that Hitler can enjoy looking at it later.

Why did important German officers try to kill their leader in the middle of a war? What led to death in the Wolf's Lair?

Adolf Hitler, aged two

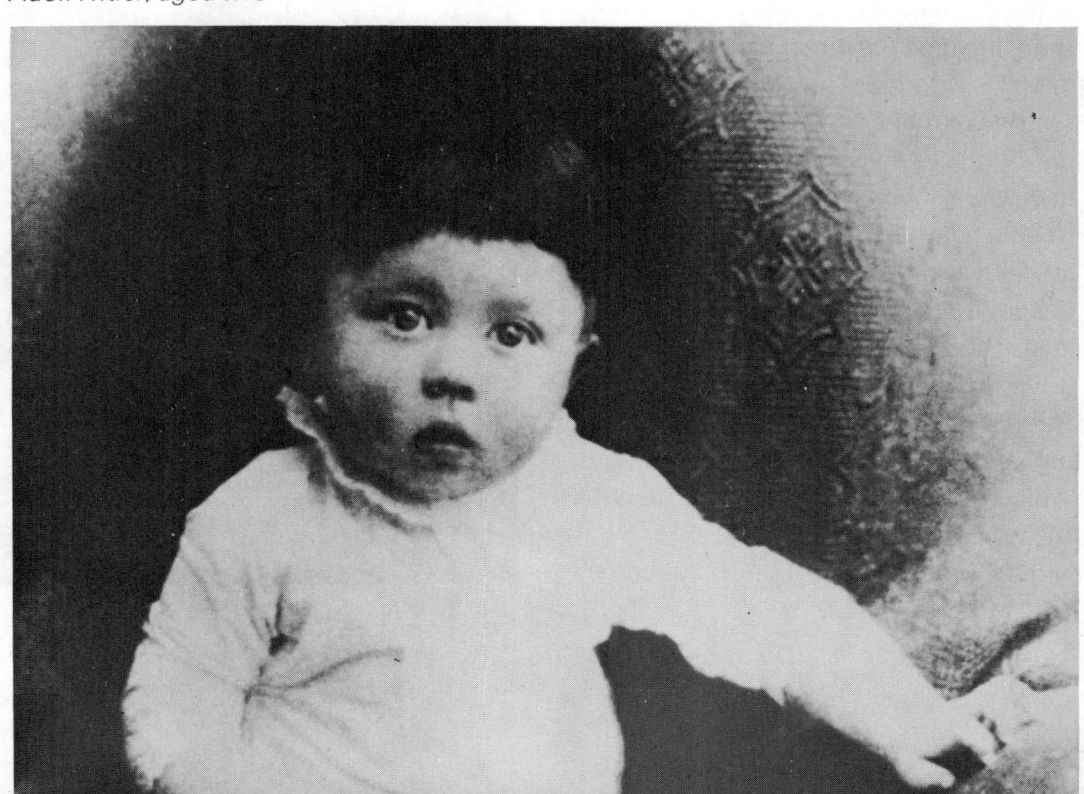

The Weimar republic

Adolf Hitler was born in Austria in 1889. He did not do well at school and when he was nineteen he went to Vienna, the Austrian capital, to be an artist. The Vienna Art Academy did not want him so he tried to earn a living by painting and selling his own postcards. He made very little at this so he was forced to do odd jobs as well. Sometimes he cleaned carpets or cleared paths of snow in the winter. He was very poor, wore ragged and dirty clothes and lived in a home for tramps.

Hitler was pleased when war came in 1914. Instead of fighting for Austria, he crossed the border and joined the German army. For much of the war he was a runner, carrying messages to the front-line. It was a dangerous job. Once he was gassed and he also won a medal, the Iron Cross, for bravery. Hitler enjoyed war; it was more exciting than life in peace-time. He left the army in 1918 with the rank of corporal.

The Germans had suffered terribly during the war. Many of their soldiers had been killed or wounded and the people at home had been starved by the allied blockade. In the end they had rebelled, forced the Kaiser (Emperor) to leave the country and set up a new government, known as the Weimar Republic after the town where its parliament met. It was this government which had decided not to carry on with the war.

The Weimar Republic soon became

Vienna, taken in the year Hitler went to live there

Hitler, sitting on the left, with fellow German soldiers

In 1919 German Communists tried to take power in Berlin. They were defeated after a week and their leaders murdered. The picture shows Communist guards during the rebellion

very unpopular. Many Germans blamed its leaders for signing the Versailles Treaty with Britain, France, Italy and the United States. By this treaty much land had been taken from Germany. In addition the Germans were forced to agree to pay for all the damage caused by the war. Even Germans who were glad the war was over felt that this treatment was unfair. They would not admit that their country alone was responsible for the war.

Other Germans were even more bitter. They said that the war had been lost because of plots by Jews and Socialists. They thought that the Weimar Republic was too soft with such people. They had also been alarmed when German Communists had started a revolution just after the war. This revolt had been crushed, but every week there were riots and fighting in the streets of German towns. In four years (1918–1922) 376 people were murdered in quarrels over politics.

One of the government's difficulties was that the new Republic was made up of a number of states. Each state had its own leaders, many of whom had different ideas of how to run the country from the government's. The Bavarian government, for instance, often disobeyed the Weimar Republic. They allowed ex-soldiers to form gangs which went around attacking Jews and Communists. When the Chief of Police in Munich, the Bavarian capital, was asked whether he knew murder gangs were loose in the city he replied, 'Yes, but not enough of them.'

Revolt in a beer-hall

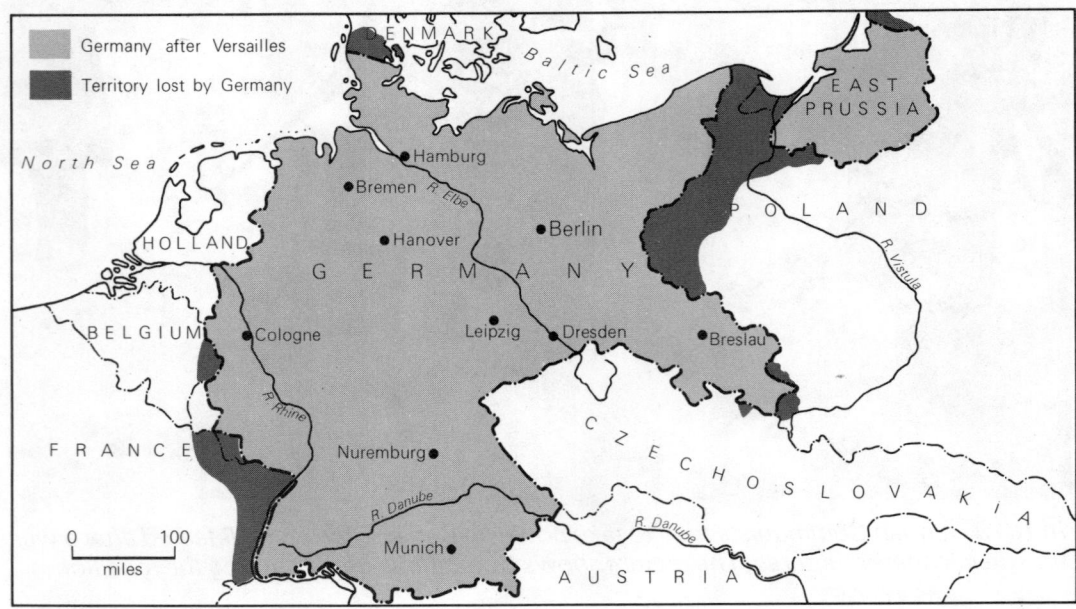

Germany after Versailles

Hitler went to Munich after the war, and very soon went into politics. Standing on chairs and tables in beer-halls, he told anyone who would listen that the German army had not been beaten fairly; it had been 'stabbed in the back' by Jewish politicians and communists who persuaded the soldiers to stop fighting. This was not true but it was what many Germans wanted to hear.

Hitler had to scream and yell to be heard above the din. If people did listen he became very excited. Spitting and shouting, his eyes blazing, he often made them burst into tears at his words. A few thought he was mad. Many more believed what he told them. Soon he had enough followers to start the German Workers' Party.

In 1920 this group joined with the National Socialist Workers' Party—the Nazis. The Nazis formed a 'Sports Section' which was supposed to protect its members. In fact, these Stormtroopers, as they were called, broke up other political meetings and beat up their opponents. The Nazi badge was a crooked cross—the swastika. The Nazi leader was Adolf Hitler.

A strict government would have put Hitler in prison. The Bavarian officials did not do so because they agreed with his hatred of Jews and Communists. Freedom went to Hitler's head. On 8 November 1923 he rushed into a Munich beer-hall, jumped on a chair

6

Hitler in prison after the Beer-hall rising

and shouted that he was going to start a revolution against the Weimar Republic. Next morning 3,000 of his Stormtroopers carrying swastika banners marched through the streets led by Hitler and one of his friends, Hermann Goering. Behind them crawled an old lorry filled with machine guns.

The marchers turned a corner to see police with rifles standing in their way. Hitler shouted, 'Surrender! Surrender!' and led his men on. The police did not move. Nobody knows who fired first but suddenly rifle shots rang out. In a few minutes the street was littered with dead, wounded and those taking cover. Hitler was dragged down by a dying friend. Goering was badly wounded.

Altogether 16 Nazis and three policemen were killed. Hitler was arrested and his party broken up.

In a well run country this would have been the end of Hitler. In Bavaria at that time he was safe. Some government ministers had liked the idea of a rebellion against the Weimar Republic. It had failed only because certain generals had backed the police against Hitler whom they looked down upon as a mere corporal! At his trial Hitler was allowed to do as he liked. He made long speeches and even interrupted witnesses. All this was reported in the newspapers. For the first time he became well known all over Germany, not just in Bavaria.

Hitler over Germany

Hitler was sentenced to five years in prison—a light sentence for such a revolt. Actually he served only nine months and spent his time pleasantly talking to visitors or writing his life story, 'Mein Kampf' (My Struggle). This book became a sort of 'Bible' to later Nazis.

When he came out of jail in December 1924 he gave up the idea of using force. It was more important, he realised, to act in a way which would make the army chiefs and rich businessmen come over to his side. The Nazis would have to fight election campaigns like other political parties.

At first the Nazis did not win many votes because the German people had recovered from their worst troubles and were doing quite well. Consequently, few wanted a change of government. In 1929, however, world trade grew less. All over Europe and America workers lost their jobs. This Slump, or Depression, hit Germany very hard. Left without jobs and often short of food, most were ready for a new form of government. Many joined the Communists but even more turned to Hitler and his Nazis. From a few thousand in 1928, Nazi votes swelled to a million by 1931.

Hitler was helped at election times by a clever journalist, Joseph Goebbels. Goebbels used every trick he knew to get more votes. Films of Hitler, records of his speeches and millions of red swastika posters were sent all over

Joseph Goebbels

Germany. Much of this was paid for by rich businessmen who feared communism. When Hitler stood for election as Chancellor (a post like prime minister in Britain) Goebbels sent him to meetings by air. He called this campaign, 'Hitler over Germany'. Thousands would gather at an open air meeting, often in a sports' stadium. They waited quietly for the sound of a plane. The roar of its engine growing louder every minute, the sudden silence after it had landed, and the appearance of Hitler in a spotlight sent them wild with excitement.

Chancellor Adolf Hitler with President Hindenburg

Such publicity brought results. By 1933 the Nazis were the largest single party in Germany. Nazi Stormtroopers marched through the streets beating up their opponents. Nazi badges, armbands and flags were seen everywhere. Only the Nazis, Hitler claimed, stood between the government and a communist revolution.

This was probably not true. But the Communist Party caused so much fear that the President of Germany, Field-Marshal Hindenberg, decided, in 1933, to take the risk of making him Chancellor—he was entitled by law to appoint a new Chancellor if he thought the country was in danger. He disliked Hitler but he preferred the Nazis to the Communists. He also thought that he could control Hitler better if he was in the government.

Hitler's first act as Chancellor seemed reasonable. He suggested there should be a general election to choose a new Reichstag (Parliament). In his speeches he said he only wanted four years of power. Behind the scenes, however, Goering promised that if the Nazis won there would be no more elections for a hundred years!

9

The Reichstag fire

A week before voting day Hitler was eating dinner with friends when his phone rang. He picked up the receiver and was told that the Reichstag building in Berlin was on fire. Jumping into a car, he drove at 60 m.p.h. to the scene. The giant dome of the building glowed red; puffs of smoke and flame curled around it. On the pavement outside stood Goering. 'This is a Communist crime against the new government', he shouted. Sure enough, a Dutch Communist, Van der Lubbe, was captured inside. In his pockets were matches and fire-lighters.

At Van der Lubbe's trial it was said that the Nazis had set fire to the Reichstag themselves so that they could blame it on to the Communists. The Nazis said the Communists had done it to start a revolution. It is now clear that it was Van der Lubbe's own idea and that no-one helped him.

The Nazis claimed that the fire proved that Germany was in real danger of a communist revolution. They said that the only way to stop this was to vote for them in the election. The final count showed that the Nazis had got 43% of all votes cast. They were joined by another party, the Nationalists, who had received 8%. Added together, this gave them the half share needed by law to govern Germany.

Once the result was known thousands of Nazis paraded past Hitler's room in the Chancellery building in Berlin, chanting slogans and waving lighted torches. In back streets storm-troopers amused themselves beating up anyone they did not like. Nazi rule had begun.

The Reichstag in flames

Roehm at a Nazi rally in 1933

The night of the long knives

Before he could do as he liked, Hitler had to deal with some of his own men. Major Ernst Roehm had led the storm-troopers for many years. He was a tough brutal man whom Hitler was supposed to like very much. Actually, Hitler did not trust the stormtrooper leader. Roehm wanted to form the stormtroopers into a new German army. Hitler was afraid this might turn the army officers against him. Roehm did not care because he hated the generals. In 1934 the two men agreed to meet to discuss the problem.

Before the meeting could start, members of Hitler's police—the S.S. Schutz Staffel (Protective Squad)—dragged some of Roehm's men out of bed and shot them outside their hotel. Roehm himself was arrested and taken to prison. He was given a revolver and told to shoot himself. When he refused he was shot. All over Germany other stormtrooper leaders were murdered.

The massacre came as a complete surprise. Very few knew why they were being killed; one man said, 'Gentlemen, I don't know what this is all about but shoot straight.' Hitler also settled one or two old scores with men he hated. A general was riddled with bullets as he opened his front door. Another man, who had helped to spoil Hitler's beer-hall revolution, was cut to pieces with pickaxes.

A few days later Hitler told the Reichstag that 61 men had been killed. There were probably more victims of the killings known as the 'Night of the Long Knives'. Two months later Hindenberg died. Now there was no one to challenge Hitler's rule.

Life under the Nazis

Hitler Youth on parade

People were not free in Hitler's Germany. There was only one political party—the Nazis. All other parties were banned. Only Nazi newspapers, radio programmes and films were allowed. Complaining about the government was an offence. Judges had to give sentences which the Nazis wanted. Often no trial was held at all and many people were imprisoned, tortured and killed without ever knowing why.

Jews, of course, were very badly treated. Laws were passed which took away all their rights as citizens. They could not marry non-Jews, could not be lawyers, doctors or teachers. Their shops and homes were wrecked by Nazi thugs. Sometimes they were made to scrub the streets, or stand against walls for hours with their hands above their heads. In certain towns German shop-keepers would not serve them with food. Soon thousands were leaving Germany.

Hitler was a good organiser. Before he came to power he had formed his

Hitler shakes hands with leaders of the Women's Labour Service, sometimes called Hitler Maids

Nazi party into a sort of government, with departments to control all sides of life. It was this ready-made organisation which now took hold of Germany. Nobody escaped the Nazi grip. Workers could not form their own trade unions; they had to join the Nazi Labour Front which was not allowed to strike. Boys joined the Hitler Youth. Although they dressed rather like Boy Scouts their ways were far different. A boy who passed a test was given a dagger, not a badge. He was taught to enjoy fighting and to hate Jews and foreigners.

Christians were told they should join the so called 'German Christian' Church. Clergymen who refused to do so were punished; some ended up in prison and one or two were shot. Women were taught it was their duty to marry and have children so that Germany could become great and powerful again. Hitler once said that women should stick to the three K's—Kinder (Children), Kerche (Church) and Kuche (Kitchen)!

The police state

Enemies of the Nazis were sent to concentration camps. These were collections of buildings surrounded by electrified fences which were guarded day and night by warders with searchlights and machine-guns. Prisoners were made to work very hard in mines and quarries. Even slight 'crimes' such as not folding a blanket properly were punished by flogging and hanging for hours by the wrists. Few men or women ever came out of these places alive; they died of torture, overwork or starvation.

Some never reached the camps at all. These people were usually dragged from their beds in the middle of the night, put in police cars and shot. Next morning the postman brought the relatives a parcel containing their ashes. This grim work was done by the Secret State Police, or Gestapo. They wore black uniforms and some had the

Inside a concentration camp

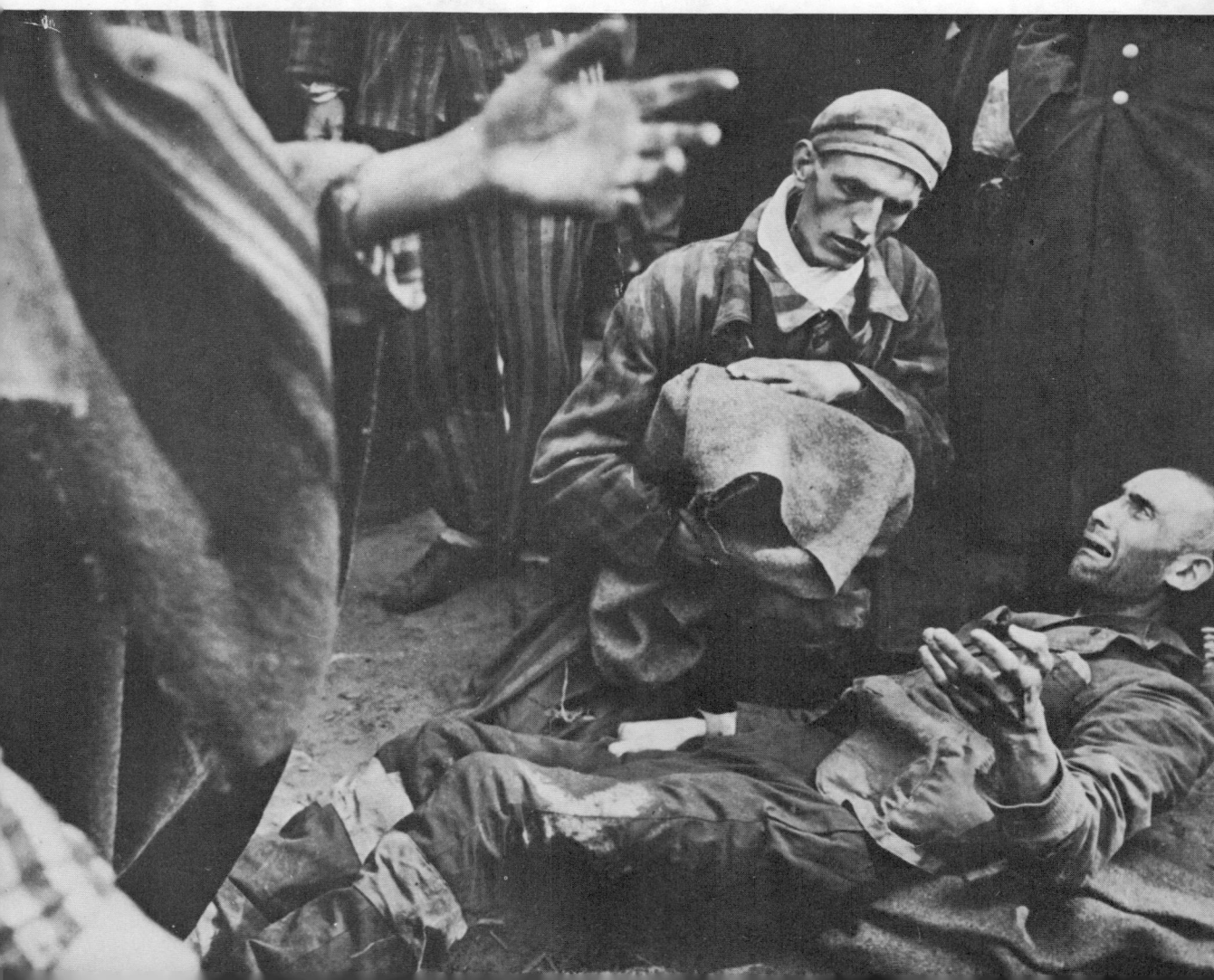

skull and crossbones for a badge. Their leader was Heinrich Himmler, a man who had once run a chicken farm.

The Gestapo used thousands of spies. Every block of flats, or row of houses, was run by a blockwarden who reported everything he heard or saw to the police. No-one could be sure he was not being watched. As well as the blockwardens, a spy might turn out to be a father, son, boss or neighbour. Even children were told it was right to tell the police what their parents said or did.

Most Germans did not mind this way of life. After all, only a few went to concentration camps at first. Furthermore, Hitler gave work to the unemployed because new roads, bridges, houses, weapons and aircraft were built. He also smashed the Communists; this pleased many well-to-do Germans who were frightened of them. Even the treatment of Jews only worried a few because in Germany Jews were not very popular.

To many Hitler seemed to be making a new, strong state out of the ruins of the old Germany. What did freedom matter if your country was great and you were well fed? In the long run, however, his success depended upon keeping certain promises to the German people.

He had told them that his government would win back all the lands taken away by the Versailles treaty. These included the Rhineland and parts of Czechoslovakia and Poland.

He had said he would bring all peoples who spoke German under his rule. This would mean taking over Austria where nearly everyone spoke German. Finally, Hitler had promised the Germans extra 'living room' in eastern Europe. This was the most dangerous proposal of all for it involved taking over several Eastern European countries and would certainly lead to a war with Russia.

It was Hitler's efforts to carry out these plans which led to the Second World War.

Heinrich Himmler takes the salute as S.S. troops march past

The Rhineland

On 7 March 1936 German troops marched into the Rhineland. The allies who won World War One had said this area was always to be *demilitarised* to protect the French from sudden attack. German officers had orders to retreat if the French army moved to stop them. Afterwards, Hitler admitted, 'The forty-eight hours after the march into the Rhineland were the most nerve-wracking of my life'.

He need not have worried. Most French generals were ready to fight to defend French territory but not to hold the Rhineland. They told their government that the French army was not fit for battle. Hitler's gamble had paid off and he felt safe enough to think of bringing Austria under his rule. Large numbers of Austrians wished to join Germany anyway. Perhaps such people could be stirred up by Nazi talk? Perhaps they could be made to riot and rebel? If so the Nazis could move in using the excuse that they had come to carry out the wishes of the people.

Austria

Inside Austria a Nazi party grew up which took its orders from Berlin. Week after week, Austrian Nazis marched through the streets, shouting that they wished to join Germany. Week after week there were riots and fights in Austrian towns. The Austrian government wondered what to do. At last they

After the occupation. Hitler drives in triumph through the streets of Vienna

After the occupation. Elderly Jews scrub pavements in Vienna watched by young Germans

made a Nazi, Seyss-Inquart, Chancellor, hoping this would stop Hitler invading their country.

Within hours of taking office Seyss-Inquart asked the German army to help bring peace and order. In March 1938 Hitler's troops occupied Austria. Quite soon Hitler himself was back in his homeland as its ruler. Tears filled his eyes as he visited his birthplace and laid flowers on his parents' graves. In the main streets crowds cheered and threw flowers. But, out of sight of pressmen and cameras, Gestapo agents carried off thousands to concentration camps. Austria's most famous politician, Dr Schuschnigg, was forced to clean lavatories. Such was life in Hitler's homeland after he had set it 'free'.

First the Rhineland and now Austria had fallen. Foreigners began to worry. In Britain, Winston Churchill said openly that Britain and France should have stopped the German army. Certainly it was not very strong at that time. During the invasion of Austria half its tanks and armoured cars broke down!

Only a few agreed. Most people dreaded the idea of another war. France had lost a million and a half men in the First World War; most of her leaders wanted peace at any price. Many British saw no real threat in Hitler's actions. Their prime minister, Neville Chamberlain, thought that the Versailles Treaty had been unfair. He thought that Hitler would be satisfied if Germany got her old lands back.

17

'Peace in our time'

Neville Chamberlain at Heston airfield after his flight to Munich. He said that his talks with Hitler would lead to 'peace in our time'

When he found that Britain and France made no moves to stop him entering Austria, Hitler felt free to turn on Czechoslovakia. There were three million Germans living in the western part of Czechoslovakia called the Sudetenland. During 1938 German Nazis in the Sudetenland complained that their people were being treated unfairly by the Czechs. This went on even after the Czech government had put most of their complaints right. It was clear that the Nazis in Germany wanted an excuse to march into Czechoslovakia.

But the Czechs had a strong army and good defences. The French had also promised to help them if they were attacked. One month after the fall of Austria, the Czechs called up their reserve soldiers and prepared for war. Hitler was taken aback because his army was not quite ready for an invasion. In public speeches he said he had meant no harm. Privately he never forgave the Czechs for standing up to him.

Neville Chamberlain, however, thought it right for the Sudetenland to go to Germany. He persuaded the French to agree with him and during the summer of 1938 Britain and France told the Czechs time after time that they must give up the Sudetenland. The Czechs did not want to; most of their railways and forts were in the area. As the quarrel grew worse, Hitler threatened the Czechs with war. Such a danger made Chamberlain go personally to see Hitler. After several talks, they met finally at Munich in September 1938.

Munich was the city where Hitler had begun his career. He had come a long way since the days when he had stood on chairs and shouted to be heard. Now he received the leaders of France, Italy and Britain as an equal. From the start he seemed to be in a bad mood. No Czech official was allowed in the room. When Chamberlain asked that Czech farmers who wished to leave the Sudetenland should be allowed to take their cattle with them, Hitler shouted, 'Our time is too valuable to be wasted on such trivialities.' After long argument he at least agreed to take over the Sudetenland peacefully by stages and not by force.

The Czechs knew they had been let down. 'We had no other choice, because we were left alone', their leader told his people. Hitler, too, was annoyed because he had really wanted the Czechs to stand up to him. Had this happened he would have had an excuse to occupy the whole country, not just

Clenched fists as German troops drive into the Sudetenland

the Sudetenland! 'That fellow Chamberlain has spoiled my entry into Prague [the Czech capital]' he grumbled. Only Chamberlain and the British people seemed to think the Munich Agreement would mean peace. Outside the prime minister's house in Downing Street, London, happy crowds sang, 'For He's a Jolly Good Fellow' and shouted 'Good old Neville'. Chamberlain leaned out of the window and said, 'My good friends, I believe it is peace in our time.'

The road to war

Chamberlain was wrong. Six months later Nazi troops marched into the rest of Czechoslovakia. The British prime minister now woke up to the danger. He called up young men for the British army—the first time Britain had ever done this in peace time. He also promised to defend any country attacked by Hitler. France did the same.

Hitler took little notice. After the Munich meeting he was sure he had nothing to fear from Britain or France. Their leaders were 'little worms' who would never fight, he said. But in March 1939 he was planning to invade Poland and another country had to be taken into account.

Russia had once ruled large parts of Poland. These lands had been lost after the First World War. The Communist ruler of Russia, Joseph Stalin, was not likely to stand by and let Poland fall into German hands. In any case, he did not like Hitler because the Nazi leader hated Communism.

Stalin knew Hitler had his eye on Poland so he tried to get an alliance with Britain and France against Germany. He offered to defend every small country between the Baltic and the Black Sea (see map) if Britain and France would do the same. The British and French leaders did not want anything to do with a Communist country. Smaller countries were sure Russia merely wished to conquer them herself. Stalin's efforts failed.

This was Hitler's chance. Britain and

Steps to War

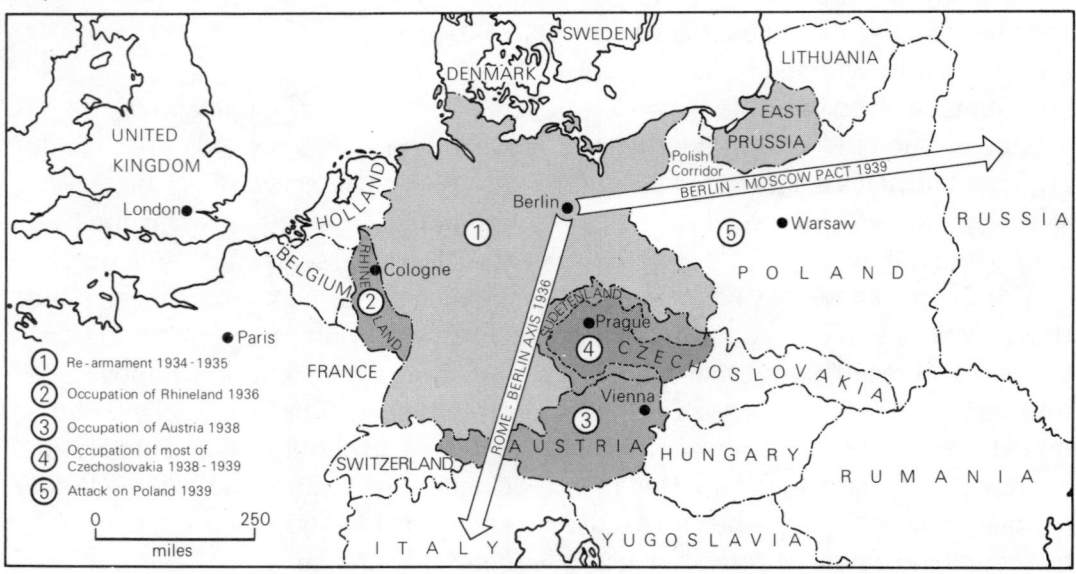

① Re-armament 1934-1935
② Occupation of Rhineland 1936
③ Occupation of Austria 1938
④ Occupation of most of Czechoslovakia 1938-1939
⑤ Attack on Poland 1939

The German Foreign Minister, Von Ribbentrop, at Berlin airport, just before flying to sign the Nazi-Soviet Pact in Moscow

France had warned him to leave Poland alone. Although he was sure they did not mean what they said, he could not risk a war with both them and Russia. On the other hand, if he could buy off Russia he could take Poland and face a war with Britain and France. The French ambassador to Germany summed up the possibility of a German attack on Poland by saying, 'Hitler will risk war if he does not have to fight Russia. If he knows he has to fight her too he will draw back.'

In July 1939 Hitler offered to sign a treaty of friendship with Russia. Stalin agreed but drove a hard bargain. Eastern Poland, Finland, Estonia and Latvia were all to go to Russia; only western Poland would come under German rule. The Nazi-Soviet Pact was signed on 24 August 1939. Neither leader trusted the other. 'After Stalin's death (he is seriously ill) we shall crush the Soviet Union', Hitler told his generals. Stalin, too, did not trust the man he privately called 'a beast'.

War

The Nazi-Soviet Pact made it certain that Germany would invade Poland. A week after it was signed, the German government radio announced that one of their frontier posts on the Polish border had been raided by the Poles. The truth was that drugged concentration camp prisoners had been dressed up in German army uniforms and shot near the border. Using this wicked trick as an excuse, Germany invaded Poland on 1 September 1939. Hitler still half believed that Britain and France would take no action. Yet two days later they declared war. He was astonished. When he was told the news he said nothing for some time. Then he asked those with him, 'What are we going to do now?' Nobody answered his question but Goering remarked, 'If we lose this war, God help us.'

Chamberlain was very unhappy.

A German panzer division with light tanks, lorries and motor cycles on the move

'Everything that I have worked for, everything I have believed in, has crashed to ruins', he told the British people. Reluctantly he led Britain for the first six months of the war. During that time the German army carried out what Hitler had suggested when he said, 'If I were going to attack an opponent I should suddenly, like a flash of lightning in the night, hurl myself upon the enemy.' The first victim was Poland.

During the First World War on the Western Front soldiers had attacked across lines of barbed wire, through land littered with shell holes. They had been shot down in thousands by well-hidden machine-gunners, or blown to pieces by shells. It was rare for the enemy to be pushed back even a few miles. Afterwards, experts tried to think of a way of getting back to a moving war. Some said that an army of tanks used like a battering ram could burst through a modern front line defence. Germany's generals decided to train a tank army to do this.

The large Polish army was trained to fight the old kind of war. The German army was led by six Panzer (Armoured) tank divisions aided by dive-bombers. With the help of sunny weather which kept the ground dry, these Panzers smashed the Poles in three weeks. The Germans called this 'Blitzkreig' which means 'lightning war'. It ended the fighting so fast that the Russians had to quickly invade Poland to get their share. Six months later the Germans occupied Norway and Denmark so that their submarines could use Norwegian ports for their raid on British merchant ships.

This second defeat was too much for the British Parliament. They sacked Neville Chamberlain and made Winston Churchill prime minister in his place. Churchill knew it would be a long, tough war. 'I have nothing to offer but blood, toil, tears and sweat,' he said. On the very day he was appointed—10 May 1940—Hitler's armies invaded France, Holland and Belgium. The most successful Blitzkreig of all had begun.

Winston Churchill in 1940

The fall of France

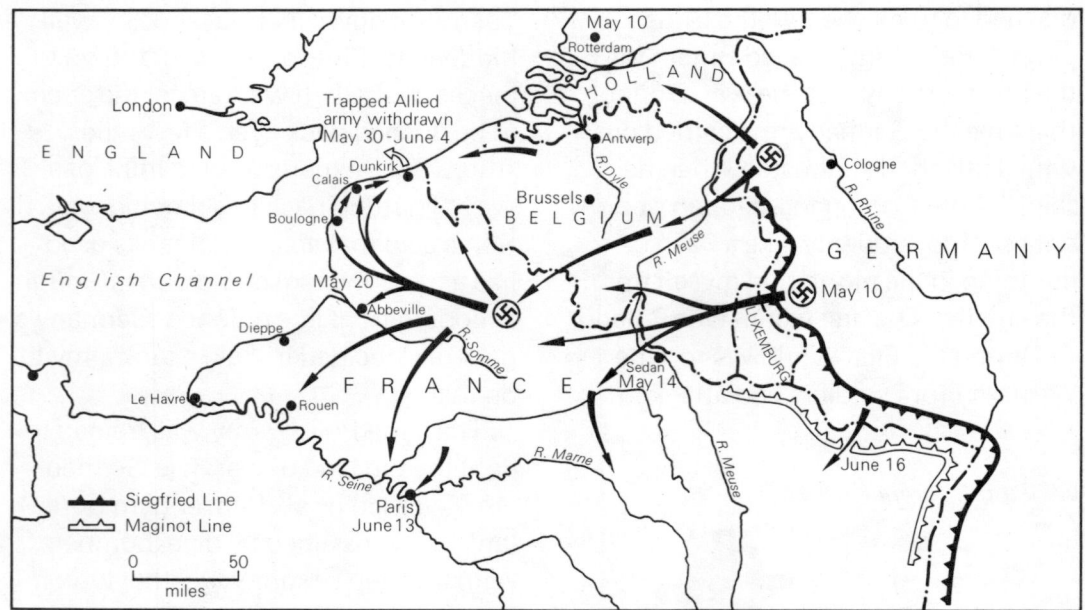

The battle for France

The next six months were a nightmare for Hitler's enemies. German paratroopers fell from the skies behind their lines, blowing up bridges and cutting telephone wires. Often they were dressed in Belgian or Dutch army uniforms to make the confusion worse. German Stuka dive-bombers screamed down to machine gun allied troops, or to lay cities like Rotterdam in Holland in ruins. In four days Holland was out of the war and Belgium soon followed.

Meanwhile an army of German tanks moved through the forests towards the French defences near Sedan (see map). It was so large that it stretched in three columns for 100 miles. Makeshift bridges were built to carry the tanks across rivers; soldiers paddled over in rubber boats. In three days' fighting this great army broke the French army once and for all. Then the Germans raced down the river valleys to the sea at Abbeville (see map) British and French troops who had rushed north to help the Belgians were cut off from France. For several weeks they tried to fight their way back. Finally, the British gave up and retreated to Dunkirk, where they were brought back to England by hundreds of small boats.

Churchill called Dunkirk 'a miracle of deliverance'. There were no miracles for the French. On 10 June 1940 Italy declared war on France because its leader, Mussolini, thought the war was over. On 14 June the Germans entered Paris. A week later French representatives surrendered to Hitler in the railway carriage where the Germans themselves had given in to the French and British in 1918.

This was the greatest moment of Hitler's life. As he walked towards the carriage he stopped to look scornfully at these words, carved by the French on a block of stone:–

'Here on the eleventh of November 1918 died the criminal pride of the German Empire—beaten by the free peoples it had tried to enslave.'

In six weeks his armies had done what the great German army of 1914 - 1918 had failed to do—beat the French. Now the shame of Germany's defeat in 1918 was wiped away.

Hitler drove a tough bargain. France was divided in two. The north was taken over by German troops. The south was formed into a separate country with its capital at Vichy. This 'Vichy Government' had very little power; it had to obey Hitler. To mark his victory, Hitler had the railway carriage taken to Germany. The stone was blown up.

Back in Berlin thousands turned out to cheer Hitler when he returned. To them it must have seemed that the war was over. Yet within a few months Hitler's air force was beaten by the R.A.F. and the Italian armies in North Africa were defeated by British troops.

Churchill had said, 'We shall never surrender' and he meant it.

Hitler and Mussolini in 1940

Hitler dances for joy after hearing of the fall of Paris

The attack on Russia

Hitler was puzzled when Churchill chose to go on fighting but he did not worry too much. Britain, in his opinion, was far too weak to hurt Germany. Only Russia seemed to stand between Germany and complete mastery of Europe. It seemed a good moment to conquer more 'living space' in the east. On 22 June 1941 Hitler's armies invaded Russia—thus breaking the Nazi-Soviet Pact which was supposed to last for 10 years.

The Russians were taken by surprise. Stalin had hoped for a long war between Britain, France and Germany which would leave all three weak whilst Russia grew strong. This hope was now shattered and he faced the whole strength of Germany alone. The outlook was grim because his own army was unprepared and badly equipped. Many of its officers were poorly trained; its aircraft were out of date; its guns often drawn by tractors and horses.

In a few months the Germans repeated their lightning war on a bigger scale in Russia. Soon the three most important Russian cities, Leningrad, Kiev and Moscow were in danger from the Germans. Millions of Russian troops were killed or captured. A happy Hitler flew over the wreckage left by the beaten Russians and said he would destroy Moscow and turn the area into a lake.

The Russians fought bravely every inch of the way back. All land likely to

German panzer troops striking towards Moscow

fall to the Germans was ruined. Its food was burned and the water poisoned; its houses pulled down and bridges wrecked. Large new armies were called up to replace the men lost. Russian factories were taken to pieces and moved to safer positions behind the Ural Mountains. Hitler did not think many Russians would fight for Stalin. But the cruelty of the Germans turned the Russians against the invader. Even Stalin was better than the Nazis.

Then the Russian winter set in. First,

Russian refugees

there was steady rain which turned the countryside into a sea of mud. One German general wrote a letter describing what it was like to fight in such conditions:—

'The infantrymen slither in the mud, while many teams of horses are needed to drag each gun forward. All wheeled vehicles sink up to their axles in the slime. Even tractors can only move with great difficulty. A large portion of our heavy artillery was soon stuck fast . . .

Snow followed the mud. The Germans were not prepared for winter; they had expected to win the war before the autumn was over. They had no warm clothes, no blankets, no sledges. Guns froze and could not be used. Fires had to be lit under tanks before they would start. Thousands of men died of cold. Thousands more lost toes, fingers or feet because of frostbite. Soup froze before it could be eaten.

Hitler felt sure he would win but some of his generals began to wonder.

27

Enter the United States

In December 1941 the U.S.A. went to war with Japan after Japanese planes had raided their fleet at Pearl Harbour in Hawaii. Hitler was already angry at the way America was helping Britain's war effort. Many U.S. weapons and even warships had been given to the British. American warships had also fired on German submarines. Since Hitler had a treaty of friendship with Japan he decided this was a suitable moment to declare war on the United States.

Hitler's action made it certain that Germany would be defeated. America was stronger than either Russia, Japan or Germany. Her war factories were too far away to be bombed; her huge armies could train without interference, her big fleet could help beat the German submarine raiders in the Atlantic. The Germans were now outnumbered; only a miracle could save them. Yet Hitler still believed that no one could beat him. Amazing success had gone to his head.

With American help, the Russians were able to equip a new army, brought from Siberia by train. These troops attacked near Moscow and almost broke the German line for good. At first, Hitler ordered his men to stand firm and fight to the last. This led to such losses that in January 1942 he had to let them go back into defensive areas called Hedgehogs. They lived like starving wolves in these camps, holding off an army which grew larger every day.

After the Japanese attack on Pearl Harbour

Alamein and Stalingrad

When spring came Hitler tried again. In Egypt his Afrika Korps moved towards the Suez Canal. In Russia the German Sixth Army turned south to grab the Russian oilfields in the Caucasus. Both attacks failed. The British beat the Afrika Korps at the battle of Alamein in October. The Sixth Army was stopped at Stalingrad in a battle which lasted five months. Inch by inch the Germans fought their way into the heart of the city. Then a fresh Russian army began to surround them.

The German commander wanted to get out before it was too late. Hitler would not let him. Because of this, 300,000 German troops were trapped in Stalingrad. They became almost savages, wrapped in rags with only

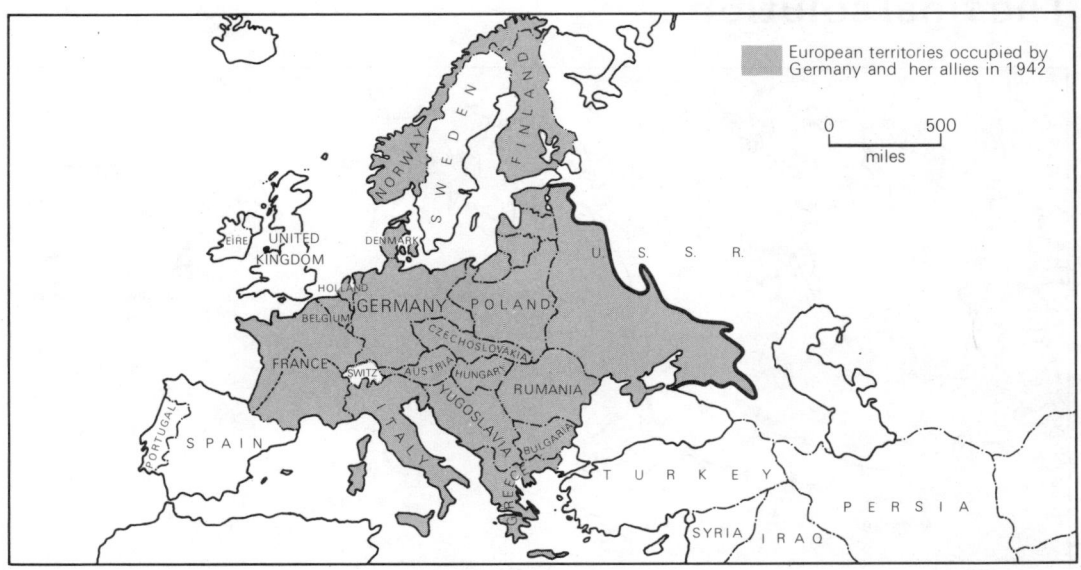

Germany's greatest expansion during the war

horse meat for food. When the Russians at last moved in, their shells turned the snowy countryside black with soot, smoke and burnt bodies. Only a third of the Sixth Army was still alive when it surrendered in January 1943.

During the next three years the Germans were beaten in one great battle after another. In 1943 American and British soldiers invaded Europe through Italy and in 1944 they landed in France. German cities were bombed day and night. The German air force and navy were almost wiped out. Attacked from Russia and France, Germany was like a nut in the jaws of a nutcracker. Hitler still thought he would be lucky. He believed fate would save him. Some of his generals thought differently. They tried to kill him in the Bomb Plot described in the first section.

The end of Mussolini. He was shot by men of the Italian resistance near the end of the war

29

The final solution

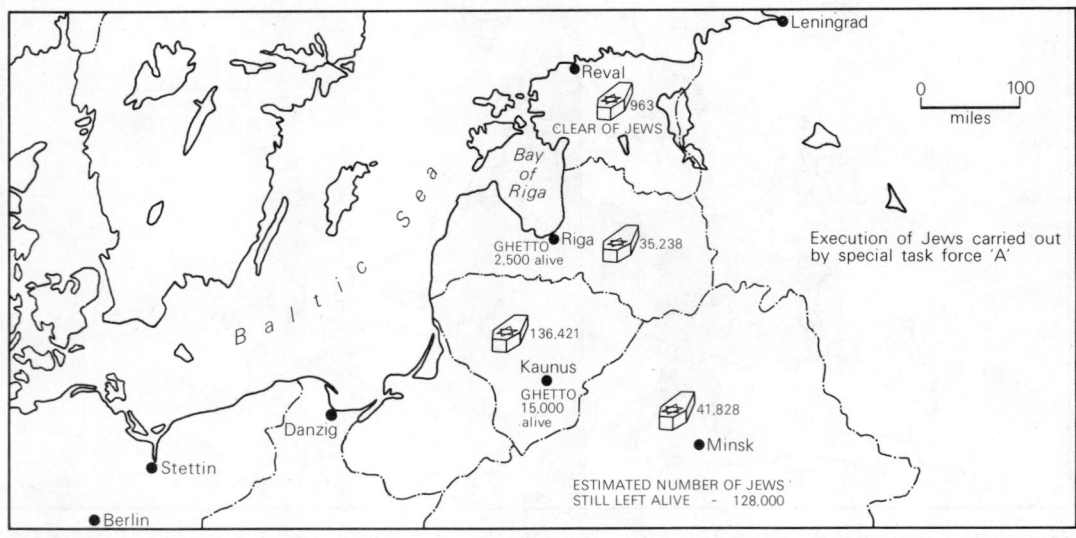

How the SS planned to finish their enemies

The soldiers who freed Europe from Hitler's grasp found dreadful signs of his cruelty.

Large numbers of Jews had lived in Poland and Russia before the German invasion. Hitler, of course, had always hated Jews. In 1942 he decided on 'the final solution' of the 'Jewish Problem', as he called it. By this he meant that they should all be killed.

The first murders were rough and ready. Jews were made to work as slaves. When they became worn out or ill they were made to dig their own graves and shot. Later shooting was stopped because bullets were scarce. At Treblinka, Auschwitz, Dachau and other camps death was produced in the same way that other factories make cars or machinery. Victims were taken to the camps in railway trucks. Once there, they were killed in gas chambers. Such chambers could kill thousands at a time. Adults knew what was going to happen to them, children did not; they were allowed to play until the last moment and then told they were going to have a shower bath. One guard said, 'We knew when the people were dead because their screaming stopped'.

Bodies were used to help the German war effort. Gold teeth were sent to the National Bank of Germany. Hair was shaved off and made into mattresses. Flesh was melted down for fat. In this way 6,000,000 Jews were killed and their bodies turned into fat, petrol and rubber.

This was the 'New Order' which Hitler made for Europe.

Jews about to board cattle-trucks which would take them to Auschwitz

Last days of Hitler

Although the Bomb Plot failed, it left Hitler very ill. His head kept on shaking; his left arm hung limp at his side. As his enemies closed in he lived in an underground room, fifty feet below the Chancellery building in Berlin. Each day he acted a little more like a madman. Brave soldiers were shot for the slightest mistake. Armies which did not exist were told to fight to the last. Towns were completely destroyed rather than let them be captured intact. If Hitler had to die he intended to destroy Germany as well!

When most of Germany was conquered he decided to kill himself. Russian guns were actually firing inside Berlin when he married Eva Braun, a woman who had loved him for many years. At the wedding meal afterwards Hitler drank champagne and talked for hours without stopping, just as he had in his young days in Munich beer halls. Early on Monday morning, 30 April 1945, he and Eva went to his room and shut the door. There was the sound of one shot and then silence.

After a few moments Goebbels opened the door. According to some accounts Hitler was lying dead on the sofa, his face dripping blood. He had shot himself through the mouth. The Russians, however, claim he poisoned himself. Near him on the floor lay Eva's body. She had been given a revolver but had used poison. Servants carried the two bodies upstairs and put them in a shell-hole. Cans of petrol were poured over them and they were set alight. As the flames roared up, Goebbels stood at attention giving the Nazi salute.

Eight days later Germany surrendered. Hitler had led his people to the worst defeat in their history.

To write

1 Make up a time line showing what happened on these dates in Hitler's life: 1889, 1914, 1920, 1933, 1934, 1936, 1938, 1939, 1940, 1944, 1945.
2 Draw or trace a map showing the lands lost by Germany in the Treaty of Versailles in 1919.
3 Draw or trace a map showing these towns; Prague, Vienna, Paris, Berlin, Moscow, Stalingrad, Munich, Dunkirk, Amsterdam, London.
4 Write two or three sentences saying what you have learned about each of these places: Versailles, Vienna, Munich, Prague, Dunkirk, Vichy, Pearl Harbour, Stalingrad.
5 What do you know about the following men: Goering, Goebbels, Hindenburg, Roehm, Neville Chamberlain, Stalin?
6 What is the English for these German words: Kampf, Reichstag, Blitzkrieg, Kinder, Panzer, Kaiser?
7 Make a list of the ways that the fighting in world war two was different from that in the first world war.

For discussion

1 Were the German officers right to try to kill Hitler. Can assassination ever be a good thing?
2 Do you think the British and French should have treated Germany so harshly after World War One?
3 Why was it so easy for Hitler to turn the German people against the Jews?
4 Would a dictatorship like Hitler's ever be possible in England?
5 Should Hitler have been allowed to take parts of Czechoslovakia in 1938?
6 Why did Britain and France not make an alliance with Russia before the Second World War?
7 Did Hitler do any good? If so, did it excuse the evil he did?

To find out

1 Ask older people what they thought of Hitler when he first came to power.
2 Read about Mussolini and the Fascists in Italy and compare them with the Nazis in Germany.
3 Find out as much as you can about the reasons behind the assassinations of Archduke Ferdinand at Sarajevo in 1919, the King of Yugoslavia in 1934, Mr Verwoerd in 1967, Martin Luther King in 1968.
4 What has happened to Czechoslovakia and Poland since 1945?
5 Look at a map of Germany today and describe the differences from a map of 1919.
6 Find out about the aircraft used in World War Two. Compare them with the aircraft of today.
7 Find out as much as you can about Rommel, Hitler's most famous general.
8 Find out as much as you can about de Gaulle's work during the Second World War.
9 What were the Nuremburg trials?
10 Why was the state of Israel founded?
11 What do these words mean: anti-semitism, appeasement, fascism, neutrality? Could they be used to describe some of the events in this book?